Origami Finger Puppets

FUN ORIGAMI FOR PINKIES, POINTERS, AND THUMBS

MUNEJI FUCHIMOTO

CONTENTS

QUARRY

LITTLE RED RIDING HOOD

"Grandmother, what big ears you have!"
"All the better to hear you with my child."

LITTLE RED RIDING HOOD
page 20

GRANDMOTHER
page 23

THE BIG BAD WOLF
page 25

TULIP
page 27

THE THREE LITTLE PIGS

"Little pig, little pig, let me come in."
"No, no, not by the hair of my chinny chin chin."
"Then I'll huff, and I'll puff, and I'll blow your house in."

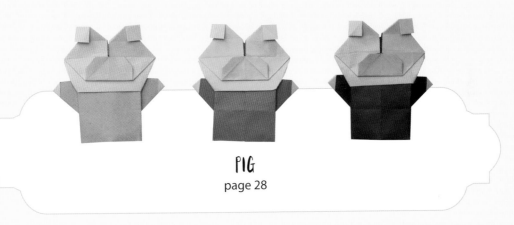

PIG
page 28

THE WOLF
page 31

HOUSE
page 34

THE LITTLE MERMAID

"I would give gladly all the hundreds of years that I have to live,
to be a human being only for one day, and to have the hope
of knowing the happiness of that glorious world above the stars."

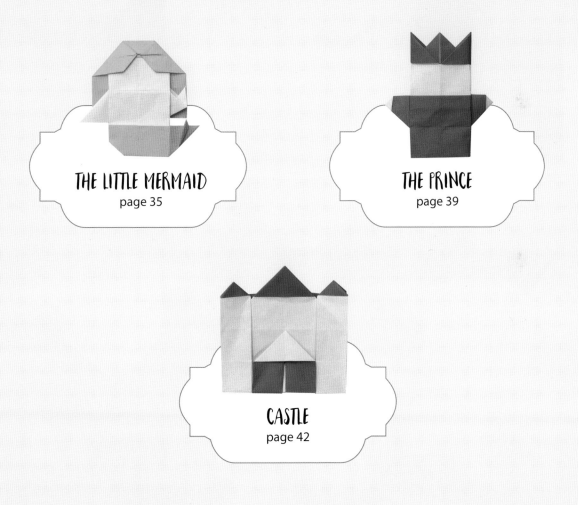

THE LITTLE MERMAID
page 35

THE PRINCE
page 39

CASTLE
page 42

THE WOLF AND THE SEVEN YOUNG KIDS

"Open the door, dear children, your mother is here,
and has brought something back with her for each of you."
"We will not open the door," cried they, "you are not our mother."

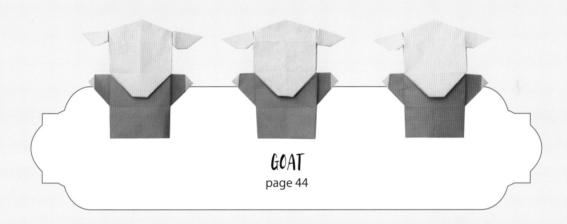

GOAT
page 44

THE WOLF
page 31

HOUSE
page 34

TOWN MOUSE AND COUNTRY MOUSE

"You may have luxuries and dainties that I have not,
but I prefer my plain food and simple life in the country
with the peace and security that go with it."

MOUSE
page 46

FLOWER
page 48

THE FROG PRINCE

"'You,' said the prince, 'have broken his cruel charm, and now I have nothing to wish for but that you should go with me into my father's kingdom, where I will marry you, and love you as long as you live.'"

THE PRINCESS
page 50

FROG
page 53

TULIP
page 27

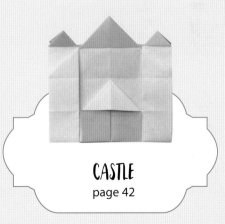

CASTLE
page 42

HAPPY HALLOWEEN!

PUMPKIN
page 55

BAT
page 57

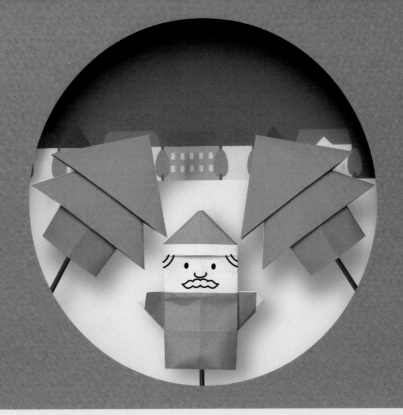

MERRY CHRISTMAS!

SANTA CLAUS
page 59

FIR TREE
page 62

BASIC FOLDS AND SYMBOLS

Valley Fold
(fold in front)

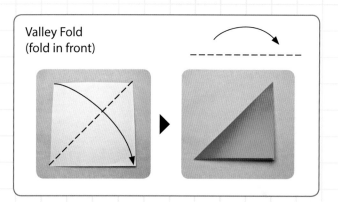

Mountain Fold
(fold behind)

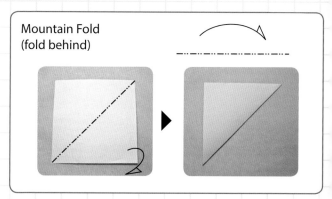

Crease in Front
(fold and unfold)

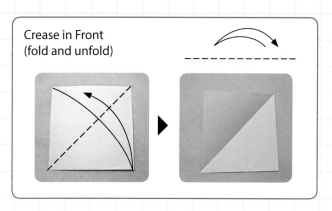

Crease Behind
(fold and unfold)

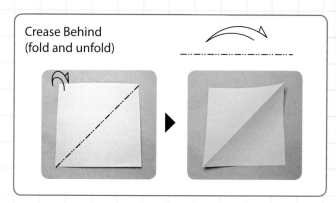

Pleat

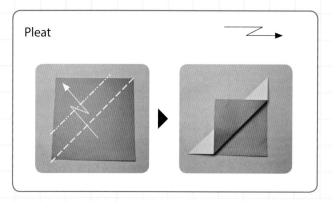

Open and Flatten

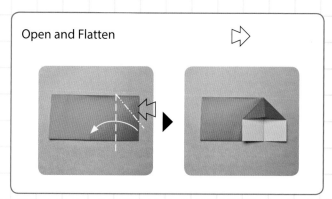

Crimp Inside

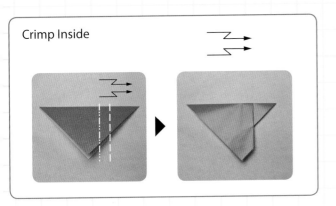

Crimp Outside

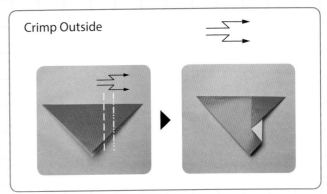

Inside Reverse Fold

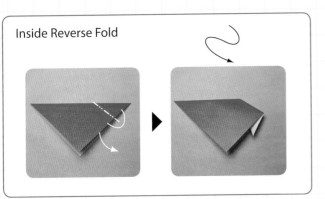

Outside Reverse Fold

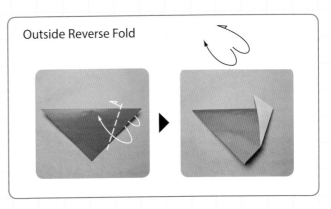

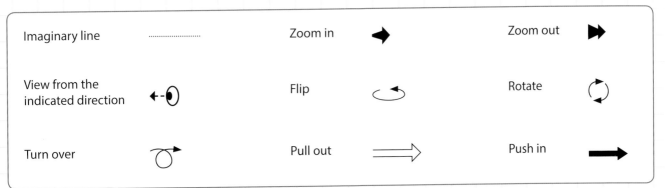

Imaginary line	....	Zoom in		Zoom out
View from the indicated direction		Flip		Rotate
Turn over		Pull out		Push in

THE BASIC STARTING SHAPE

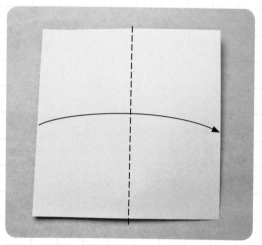

1 Fold in half from edge to edge.

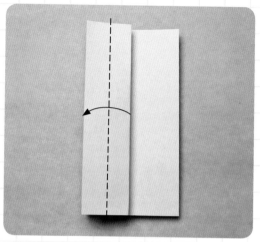

3 Fold the top layer in half again.

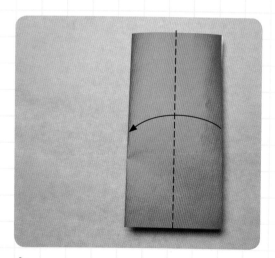

2 Fold the top layer in half

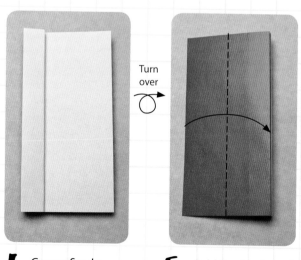

Turn over

4 Crease firmly.

5 Fold the top layer in half.

Most of the finger puppets in this book start with this basic shape.
Master this technique before getting started with one of the projects.

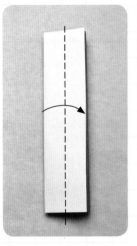
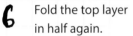

6 Fold the top layer in half again.

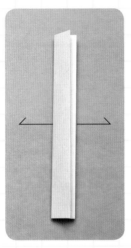

7 Unfold everything.

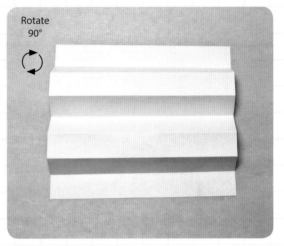

Rotate 90°

9 Repeat steps 1–7.

8 The vertical creases are complete.

The basic starting shape is complete!

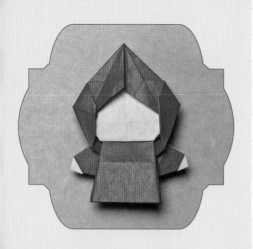

LITTLE RED RIDING HOOD

Shown on page 2

Difficulty ★★★★☆

Getting Started
Complete steps 1–5 of Santa Claus on pages 59–60.

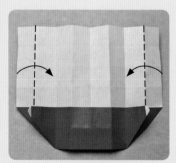

1 Fold along the two outermost vertical creases.

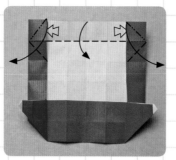

2 Open both top corners and flatten along the top horizontal crease.

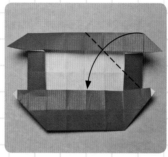

3 Fold diagonally, bringing the top right corner to the center.

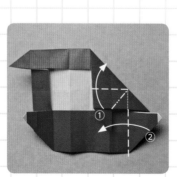

4 Open the top right corner while flattening the bottom right corner to the left.

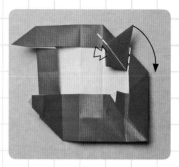

5 Open the top right corner and flatten to the right.

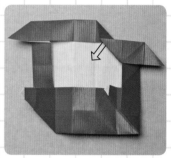

6 Pull out the inner layer.

7 View from the top.

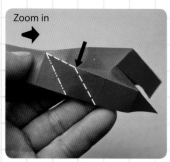

8 Reverse the creases as shown and collapse back down.

11 Repeat steps 3–10 on the left side.

14 Fold all layers back to the right.

9 In progress view of the collapsing process used in step 8.

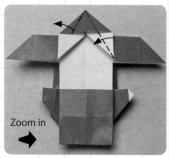

12 Open the top layer and flatten along the fold lines shown.

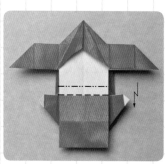

15 Pleat through all layers.

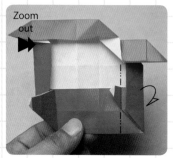

10 Fold the right edge behind.

13 Fold the inner edge to the left as shown.

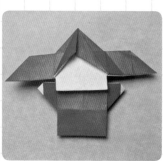

16 Completed view of step 15.

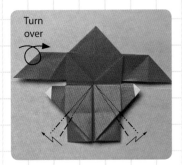

17 Pleat the arm flaps down by pivoting around the center point.

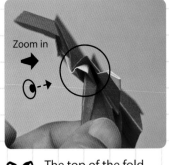

20 The top of the fold will form a triangle as shown. Repeat on the left side.

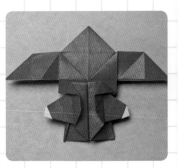

23 Completed view of step 22.

18 Completed view of step 17.

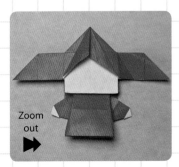

21 Completed view of step 20.

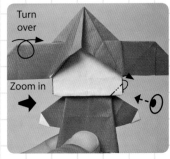

24 Reverse fold a corner inside.

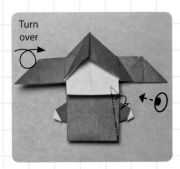

19 Fold the right edge behind.

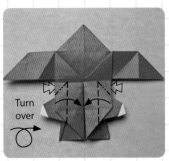

22 Fold the sides into the center while opening and flattening triangles at the top.

Side view of step 24.

25 Repeat step 24 on the left side.

28 Fold the edge behind into the gap between the body and the arm.

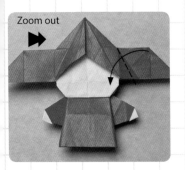

Zoom out

26 Fold diagonally.

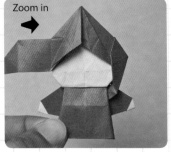

Zoom in

29 Repeat steps 26–28 on the left side.

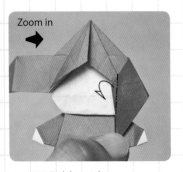

Zoom in

27 Fold inside.

Little Red Riding Hood is complete!

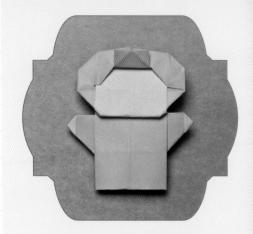

GRANDMOTHER

Shown on page 2

Difficulty ★★★☆☆

Getting Started
Complete steps 1–5 of Santa Claus on pages 59–60.

1 Fold downward along the top horizontal crease.

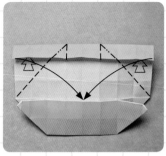

2 Open each side of the top layer and flatten down along the creases shown.

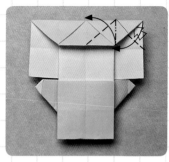

5 Open and flatten along the creases shown.

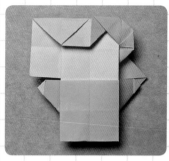

8 Repeat steps 5–7 on the left side.

3 Pleat each side behind while opening the top layers out.

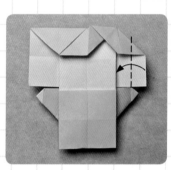

6 Fold the right edge to the next vertical edge.

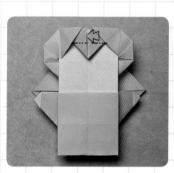

9 Open along the lines shown.

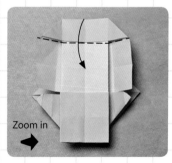

Zoom in

4 Fold downward.

7 Fold diagonally, tucking the flap behind the head.

Zoom in

10 Flatten upward to fold a rectangle.

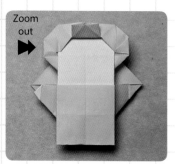

11 Completed view of step 10.

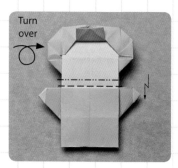

14 Pleat through all layers.

THE BIG BAD WOLF

Shown on page 2

Difficulty ★★☆☆☆

Getting Started
Complete steps 1–3 of Goat on pages 44–45.

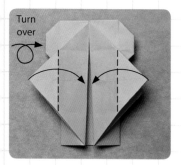

12 Fold the points to the center.

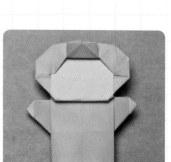

15 Inside reverse fold the bottom two corners of the face.

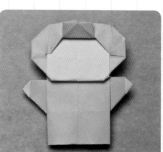

13 Completed view of step 12.

Grandmother is complete!

1 Completed view of steps 1–3 on pages 44–45.

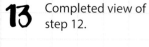

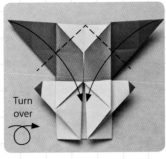

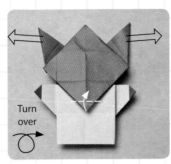

Zoom in

2 Fold diagonally, bringing the corners to the center.

5 Fold the tip of the nose upward. Unfold the ears.

Close up view of the folding process in step 7.

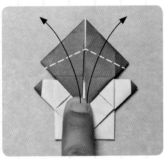

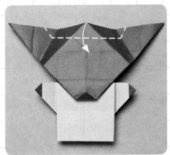

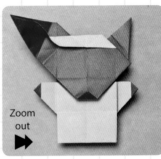

Zoom out

3 Fold diagonally to create the ears.

6 Fold the top layer down along a horizontal line, folding only the middle section.

8 Fold the left ear in the same way.

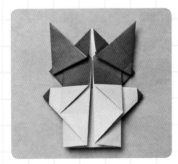

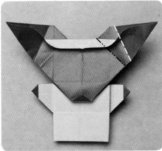

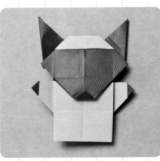

4 Completed view of step 3.

7 Collapse the right ear back behind along the existing creases.

The Big Bad Wolf is complete!

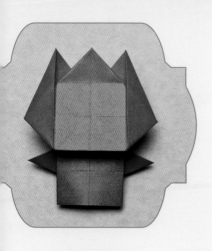

TULIP

Shown on pages 2 and 12

Difficulty ★★☆☆☆

Getting Started
Complete step 1, then steps 3–5 of Santa Claus on pages 59–60 (skip step 2).

1 Pleat each side along the creases shown.

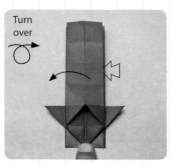

Turn over

2 Unfold the right side and flatten to the left.

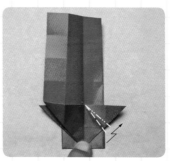

3 Pleat down diagonally.

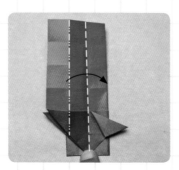

4 Reform the pleat that was unfolded in step 2.

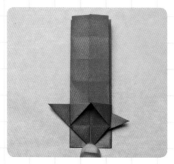

5 Repeat steps 2–4 on the other side.

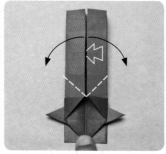

6 Open along the creases shown. Note: The model will not lie flat.

7 Fold the corners inside and to the center.

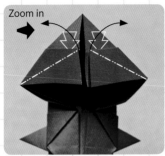

8 Pull the two corners up and out diagonally as shown.

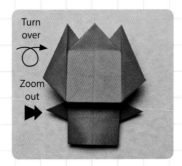

The tulip is complete!

9 Flatten by pleating down along the creases shown.

10 Completed view of step 9.

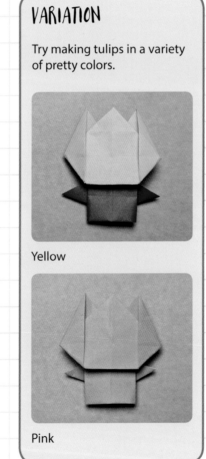

VARIATION

Try making tulips in a variety of pretty colors.

Yellow

Pink

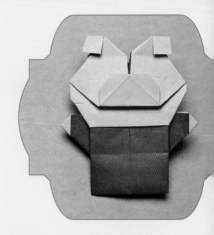

PIG

Shown on page 4

Difficulty ★★★★☆

Getting Started
Complete steps 1–5 of Santa Claus on pages 59–60.

1 Crease as shown, making creases in the middle of squares from previous creases.

2 Fold in along the outermost vertical crease on each edge.

3 Pleat in front.

4 The next step will focus on the area inside the square.

Zoom in

5 Pleat the lower layer behind without folding the top layer. Note: The model will not lie flat.

6 Push in the bottom edge of the upper layer as shown.

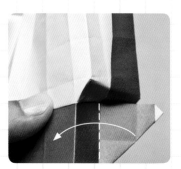

7 Fold the arm to the left.

8 Pleat the remaining paper forward along the lines shown.

Back view of step 8.

9 Repeat steps 5–8 to fold the other arm in the same way.

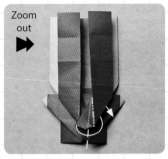

10 Inside reverse fold.

13 Completed view of step 12.

16 Fold downward.

11 Tuck hidden flap between layers that were reverse folded in step 10.

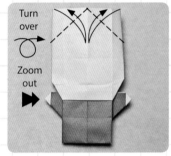

14 Fold the corners to the center and unfold.

17 Fold and unfold.

12 Fold the thick flap through many layers and into the pocket as shown.

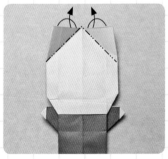

15 Inside reverse fold the two corners.

18 Open the two inner edges and flatten outward to form a rectangle.

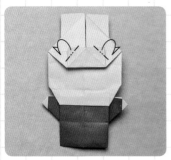

19 Fold the tip of each corner behind.

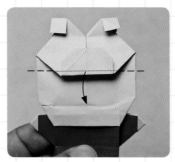

22 Pleat the head and nose down as shown.

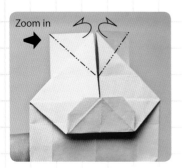

Zoom in ➤

20 Fold behind.

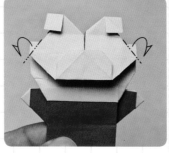

23 Fold the upper corners of the face behind.

21 Open the tip of each ear and flatten into a square.

The pig is complete!

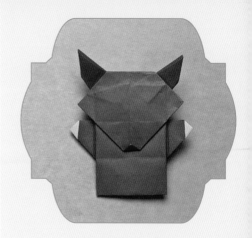

THE WOLF

Shown on pages 4 and 8

Difficulty ★★★☆☆

Getting Started
Complete steps 1–5 of Santa Claus on pages 59–60.

1 Fold the the top corners diagonally, aligning the edges with the creases.

2 Fold the edges in along the outermost vertical creases.

5 Crease along the lines shown, and then collapse along the existing creases as shown.

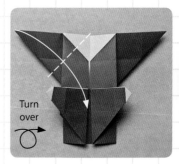

7 Fold diagonally, bringing the left corner to the center.

Turn over

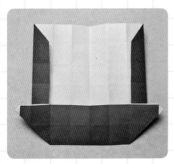

3 Completed view of step 2.

In progress view of the collapsing process used in step 5.

8 Completed view of step 7. Lift the flap and look inside.

Turn over

4 Crease along the lines shown.

6 Completed view of step 5.

Zoom in

9 Fold the hidden inner point behind.

10 Repeat steps 7–9 on the right side.

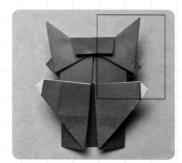

13 The next step will focus on the area inside the rectangle (see photo).

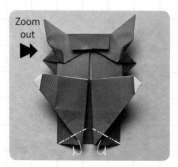

Zoom out ▶▶

16 Fold the corners behind.

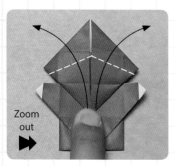

Zoom out ▶▶

11 Fold diagonally.

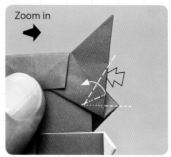

Zoom in ▶

14 Open and flatten along the lines shown.

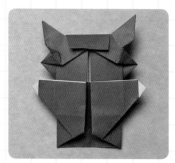

17 Completed view of step 16.

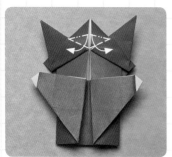

12 Open the two center edges and flatten into a rectangle.

15 Repeat step 14 on the left side.

Turn over ↻

The Wolf is complete!

HOUSE

Shown on pages 4 and 8

Difficulty ★★☆☆☆

Getting Started
Start from the basic starting shape (refer to page 18).

1 Fold the bottom horizontal crease behind.

2 Fold each edge behind along the second vertical crease.

3 Crease diagonally.

4 Collapse along the existing creases as shown.

Zoom in

5 Unfold the two corners.

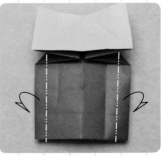

6 Fold each edge behind to meet the first vertical crease line.

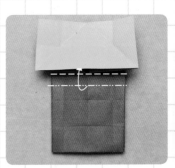

7 Pleat upward and tuck the excess paper under the roof.

8 Fold the top corners behind.

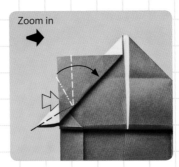

Zoom in ➡

11 Fold along the lines shown.

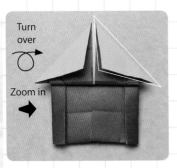

Turn over

Zoom in ➡

9 Insert the enclosed area into the bottom gap.

12 Completed view of step 11.

10 Fold diagonally.

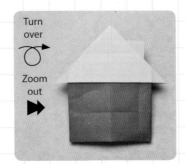

Turn over

Zoom out ⏩

The House is complete!

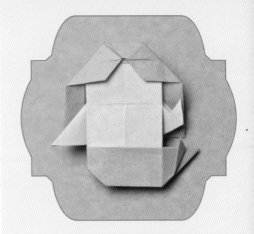

THE LITTLE MERMAID

Shown on page 6

Difficulty ★★★★☆

Getting Started
Start from the basic starting shape (refer to page 18).

1 Fold in along the top and bottom horizontal creases.

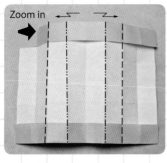

2 Pleat.

5 View from the top right.

8 Repeat steps 5–7 on the other side.

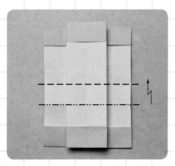

3 Pleat through all layers.

6 Open slightly.

9 Open the top layer and flatten into a triangle.

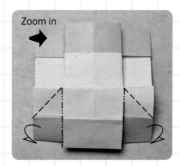

4 Fold each edge behind while flattening the top of each edge into a triangle.

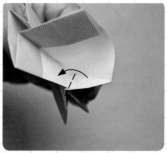

7 Fold the inner corner up without opening the base of the arm to lock the layers together.

10 Fold the corner inside.

11 Inside reverse fold the small corner as shown.

14 Open slightly and view from the right.

17 Fold diagonally.

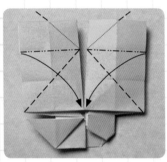

12 Fold the side edges down and collapse along the creases shown.

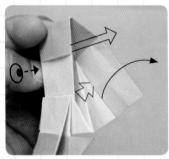

15 Pull out the inner edge of the paper and flatten.

18 Repeat steps 14–17 on the left side.

13 Completed view of step 12.

16 Fold the right edge to the side of the face.

19 Open the center edges and flatten into a rectangle.

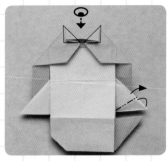

20 Inside reverse fold the right arm. Hide the marked triangles under the next layer of paper below.

22 Inside reverse fold along the creases shown.

25 View from the front.

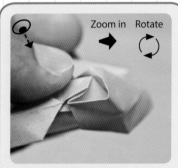

Zoom in   Rotate

In progress view, hiding the small triangles below the next layer.

23 Pull out the edge of the paper by reversing the creases as shown.

26 Fold one flap up diagonally.

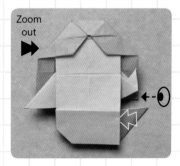

Zoom out

21 Lift the top layer and look inside.

24 Flatten down, folding along the line shown.

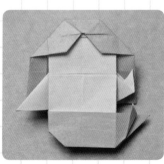

27 Completed view of step 26.

28 Lift the top layer and look inside.

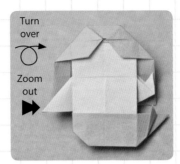

The Little Mermaid is complete!

29 Fold the hidden corner behind as shown.

VARIATION

If you want to transform the Little Mermaid into a human, just skips step 9–11 and steps 21–30.

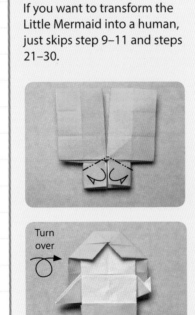

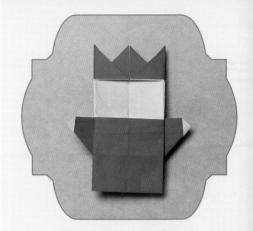

THE PRINCE

Shown on page 6

Difficulty ★★☆☆☆

Getting Started
Start from the basic starting shape (refer to page 18).

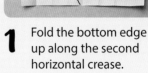

30 Close and flatten.

1 Fold the bottom edge up along the second horizontal crease.

2 Fold the left corner to the center of the first grid square. Repeat on the right corner.

3 Complete steps 3–5 of Santa Claus on page 60.

4 Fold diagonally, bringing the corners to the center.

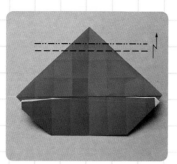

5 Pleat the topmost horizontal crease on to the horizontal crease second from the top.

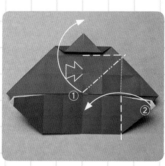

6 Fold corner 1 upward while flattening the right edge 2 into the center.

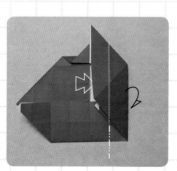

7 Fold the right edge behind as shown. Note: The model will not lie flat.

8 Fold the top edges as shown.

9 Repeat steps 6–8 on the left.

10 Fold behind.

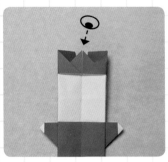

11 Look into the top.

13 Repeat on the right.

In progress view of step 15.

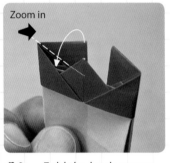

12 Fold the back corner inside.

14 Pleat down.

In progress view of step 12.

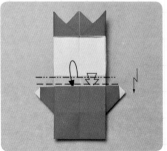

15 Open the shirt and insert the pleat from step 14 inside.

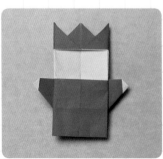

16 Completed view of step 15.

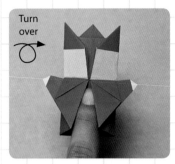

17 Insert your finger into the back of the puppet as shown.

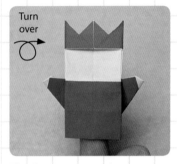

The Prince is complete!

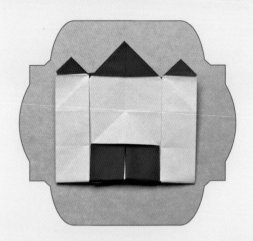

CASTLE

Shown on pages 6 and 12

Difficulty ★★★☆☆

Getting Started
Start from the basic starting shape (refer to page 18).

1 Fold down along the top horizontal crease.

2 Fold the top corners backward.

3 Crease along the lines shown.

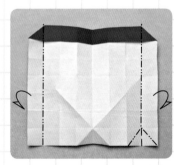

4 Fold the side edges behind along the outermost vertical creases. Form a reverse fold in the bottom right corner.

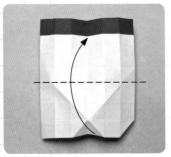

5 Fold upward along the third horizontal crease from the bottom.

7 Fold the bottom left flap behind.

In progress view of step 9.

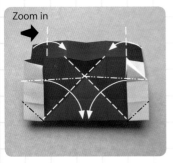

6 Collapse along the existing creases as shown.

8 Repeat step 7 on the right, but pull the marked triangle to the front through the slit in the center.

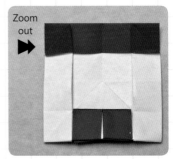

10 Completed view of step 9.

In progress view of step 6.

9 Insert the white triangle in between the layers of the blue square on the left.

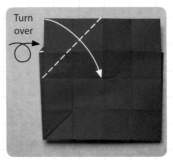

11 Fold diagonally, aligning the top left corner with the second horizontal crease.

12 Lift the top layer and look inside.

14 Repeat steps 11–13 on the right.

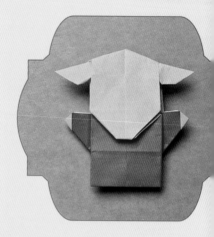

GOAT

Shown on page 8

Difficulty ★★☆☆☆

Getting Started
Complete steps 1–5 of Santa Claus on pages 59–60.

Zoom in ➡

13 Open and flatten along the lines shown.

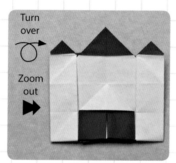

Turn over ↻

Zoom out ⏩

The Castle is complete!

In progress view of step 13.

1 Fold behind and unfold along the creases shown.

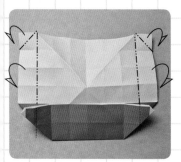

2 Fold behind the top corner grid squares in half diagonally, and then fold each edge behind along the outermost vertical creases.

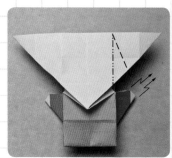

4 Crimp the right corner inside by rotating around the top point as shown.

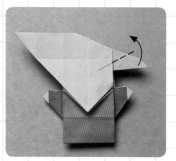

7 Fold the right corner up diagonally through all layers.

3 Collapse along the existing creases as shown.

5 Fold behind at an angle.

8 Pleat through all layers to rotate the ear back down.

In progress view of step 3.

6 Fold the exposed corner forward and tuck inside.

9 Repeat steps 4–8 for the left ear.

10 Fold the nose tip behind.

The Goat is complete!

MOUSE

Shown on page 10

Difficulty ★★★☆☆

Getting Started
Complete steps 1–3
of the Goat on pages
44–45.

1 Completed view of step 3 from page 45.

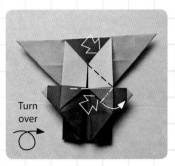

Turn over

2 Open slightly along the lines shown.

3 Fold the top right corner to the left as shown.

4 Open the layers at the bottom and flatten the left side down as shown.

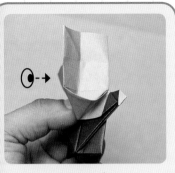

In progress view of step 4.

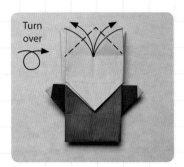

7 Fold the corners to the center line and unfold.

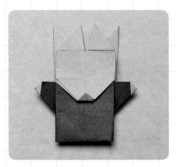

10 Completed view of step 9.

5 Fold the small triangle inside as shown. Repeat steps 2–5 on the left.

8 Fold the top edge inside while flattening along the creases made in step 7.

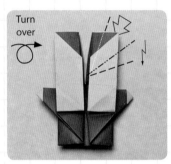

11 Pleat the top layer down and flatten diagonally to form the ear.

6 Completed view of step 5.

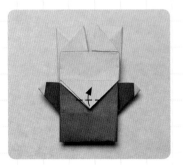

9 Fold the nose tip up.

12 Inside reverse fold the right corner.

13 Repeat steps 11–12 on the left.

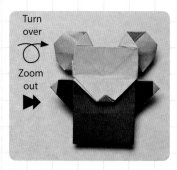

Turn over

Zoom out

The Mouse is complete!

FLOWER

Shown on page 10

Difficulty ★★★☆☆

Getting Started
Start from the basic starting shape (refer to page 18).

1 Fold the bottom corners behind.

2 Fold the bottom edge behind along the first horizontal crease.

3 Fold the side edges to the center while collapsing the reverse folds on the top as shown.

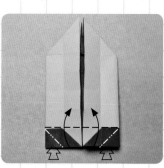

4 Fold up the top layer on each side and flatten each side into a triangle.

5 Inside reverse fold the corners as shown.

In progress view of step 7.

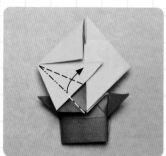

10 Fold to align the bottom third with the center.

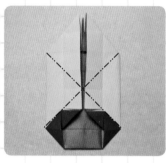

6 Fold behind and unfold as shown.

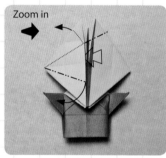

Zoom in

8 Open the left side and flatten the corner symmetrically to the right.

11 Fold to the left.

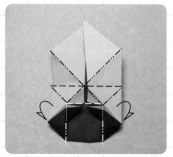

7 Fold the bottom two sides behind while collapsing along the creases shown.

9 Open the layers at the top and flatten the top section into a triangle.

12 Repeat steps 8–11 on the right.

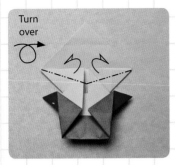

Turn over

13 Fold the two corners inside as shown.

14 Completed view of step 13.

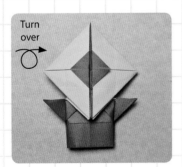

Turn over

The Flower is complete!

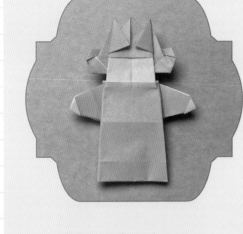

THE PRINCESS

Shown on page 12

Difficulty ★★★★☆

Getting Started
Start from the basic starting shape (refer to page 18).

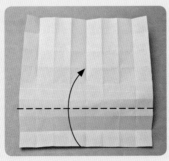

1 Fold the bottom edge up to meet the third horizontal crease from the top.

Zoom in

2 Fold the left corner to the center of the first grid square.

3 Pinch the corner in half and fold it to the left along the creases shown.

4 In progress view of step 3.

5 Repeat steps 2–4 on the right.

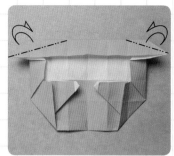

8 Fold behind and unfold along the creases shown.

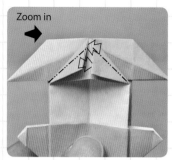

11 Open the layers in the center on each side and flatten them upward.

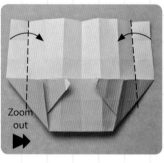

6 Fold in along the outermost vertical creases.

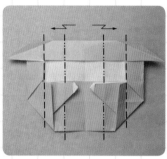

9 Pleat as shown while swinging the hands outward.

12 Completed view of step 11.

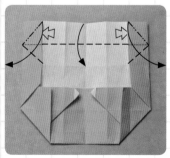

7 Open the top corners outward and fold the top edge down along the first horizontal crease.

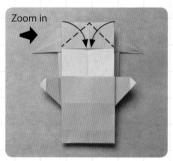

10 Fold diagonally to align the corners at the center.

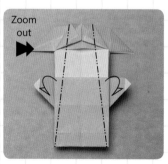

13 Fold the sides behind and inside as shown.

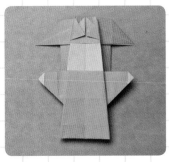

14 Completed view of step 13.

17 Fold in along the existing crease.

20 Repeat steps 15–19 on the left.

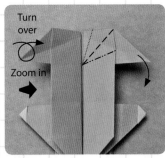

15 Pull the corner down while pleating the top layer as shown.

18 Outside reverse fold.

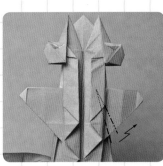

21 Pleat only the arm flap down as shown.

16 Fold the right edge to the center. Open and flatten the top into a triangle.

19 Fold the flap behind and weave it back to the front.

22 Thin the arm by folding the bottom edge up and flattening the left side into a triangle.

23 Repeat steps 21–22 on the left.

26 Fold the sides of the dress back behind.

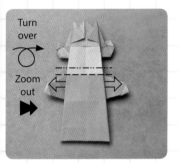

Turn over

Zoom out

24 Pleat the neck down and unfold. Pull out the paper along the sides of the dress.

Zoom out

The Princess is complete.

Zoom in

25 Tuck the pleat into the top of the dress.

FROG

Shown on page 12

Difficulty ★★★★☆

Getting Started
Complete steps 1–16 of the Pig on pages 28–30.

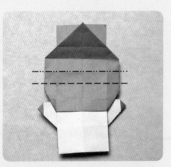

1 Pleat through all layers as shown.

2 Fold the two corners behind.

5 Open the layers and flatten into a square.

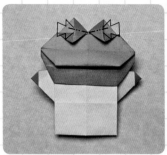

8 Open the eyes slightly so they are 3–D.

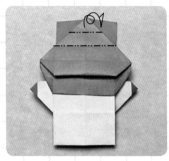

3 Fold the top corner behind twice as shown.

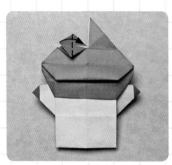

6 Fold toward the center.

9 Completed view of step 8.

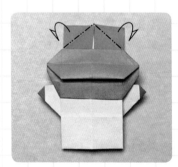

4 Fold the two top corners behind.

7 Repeat steps 5–6 on the right.

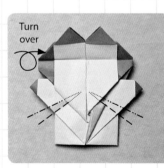

10 Pleat only the arm flaps down as shown.

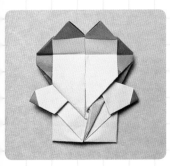

11 Completed view of step 10.

Turn over

The Frog is complete!

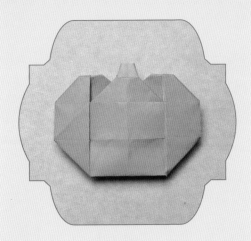

PUMPKIN

Shown on page 14

Difficulty ★★★☆☆

Getting Started
Start from the basic starting shape (refer to page 18).

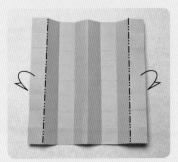

1 Fold behind along the outermost vertical creases.

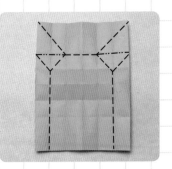

2 Collapse along the creases shown.

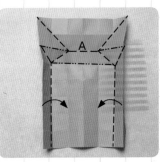

A

3 In progress view of step 2. Fold the side edges in toward the center. Pleat the top so point A becomes hidden.

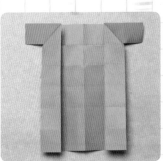

4 Completed view of step 3.

5 Fold diagonally.

8 Inside reverse fold.

11 Fold the bottom edge up along the third horizontal crease from the bottom.

6 Open the top layer and flatten the bottom paper as in step 7.

9 Completed view of step 8. Flatten back down.

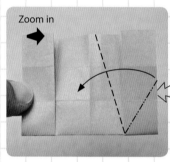

12 Open the right edge diagonally to the left and flatten the bottom into a triangle.

7 Lift the flap and look inside.

10 Repeat steps 5–10 on the left.

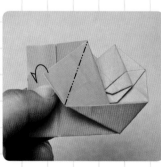

13 Fold behind.

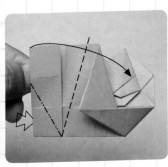

14 Repeat step 12 on the left.

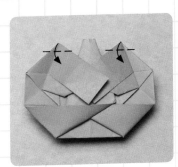

17 Fold the top two corners down.

15 Tuck the excess paper behind.

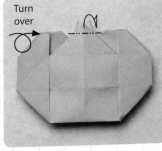

Turn over

18 Fold the center point behind.

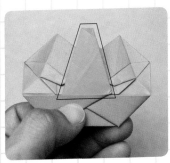

16 Move the layers behind the stem to the front.

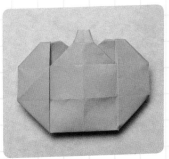

The Pumpkin is complete!

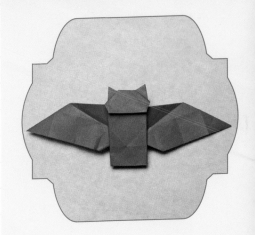

BAT

Shown on page 14

Difficulty ★★★☆☆

Getting Started
Start from the basic starting shape (refer to page 18).

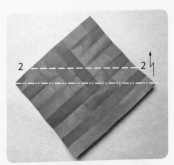

1 Pleat diagonally along the center. Make the second pleat line two grid units away.

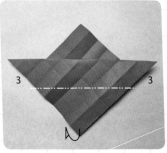

2 Fold the bottom corner behind three grid units below the diagonal.

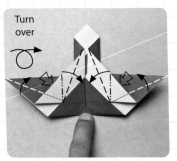

5 Fold the sides to the center and flatten the outside edges up as shown.

8 Fold the top corner down.

3 Pleat.

6 Pleat behind through all layers.

9 Pleat corners in front.

4 Completed view of step 3.

7 Open outward along the lines shown.

10 Completed view of step 9.

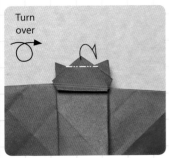

11 Fold the top corner behind.

14 Repeat steps 12–13 on the left.

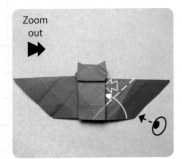

12 Open the side of the body slightly and fold the right wing up. Look inside.

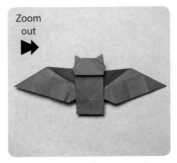

The Bat is complete!

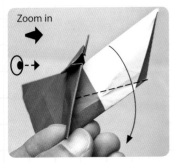

13 Fold the right wing back down as shown.

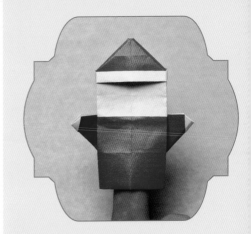

SANTA CLAUS

Shown on page 15

Difficulty ★☆☆☆☆

Getting Started
Start from the basic starting shape (refer to page 18).

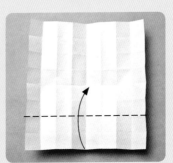

1 Fold up along the second horizontal crease from the bottom.

2 Fold the left corner to the center of the first grid square. Repeat on the right corner.

Zoom in ➡

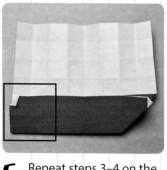

5 Repeat steps 3–4 on the left.

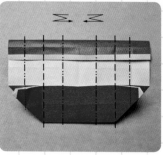

8 Pleat the sides in and out evenly along the creases as shown.

Zoom out ⏩

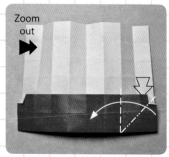

3 Open the corner to the left and flatten to form a triangle.

6 Fold the top edge down to meet the third horizontal crease from the top.

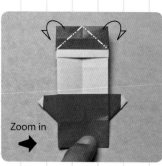

Zoom in ➡

9 Fold the top layer of each corner inside.

4 Fold to the right along the line shown.

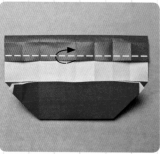

7 Fold the edge up ⅓ of the way to the first horizontal crease.

10 Fold the bottom layer of the corners forward and tuck inside.

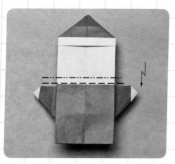

11 Pleat forward.

Rotate

In progress view of step 12.

15 Completed view of step 14.

12 Open the shirt and insert the pleat from step 11 inside.

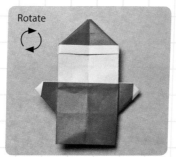

Rotate

13 Completed view of step 12.

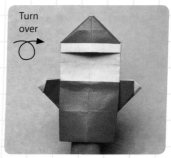

Turn over

Santa Claus is complete!

Folding the corners of the face may make it easier to insert the head into the shirt.

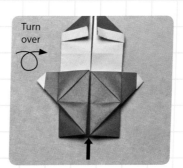

Turn over

14 To use the finger puppet, insert your finger into the area indicated by the arrow.

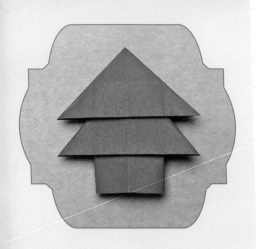

FIR TREE

Shown on page 15

Difficulty ★☆☆☆☆

Getting Started
Start from the basic starting shape (refer to page 18).

1 Fold in along the second vertical crease from each edge.

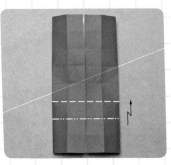

2 Pleat.

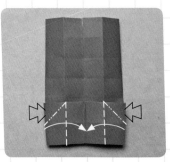

3 On each side, open and fold to the center, forming triangles.

4 Pleat.

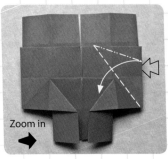

Zoom in ➡

5 Open and fold along the line shown.

6 Fold diagonally.

7 Open and fold along the line shown.

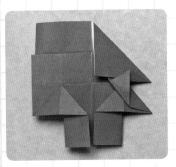

8 Repeat steps 5–7 for the left side.

9 Completed view of step 8.

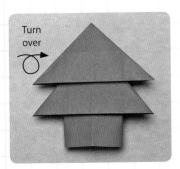

Turn over

The Fir Tree is complete!

ABOUT THE AUTHOR

Muneji Fuchimoto is the president and art director of graphic design firm SCOG Design Inc. Inspired by a project his son made in his kindergarten class, Fuchimoto began creating original origami designs in 2005. He is the author of multiple origami books and is known for his unique robot and animal designs.

Quarto is the authority on a wide range of topics.

Quarto educates, entertains and enriches the lives of our readers—enthusiasts and lovers of hands-on living.

www.QuartoKnows.com

First published in the United States of America in 2016 by
Quarry Books, an imprint of
Quarto Publishing Group USA Inc.
100 Cummings Center
Suite 406-L
Beverly, Massachusetts 01915-6101
Telephone: (978) 282-9590
Fax: (978) 283-2742
QuartoKnows.com
Visit our blogs at QuartoKnows.com

10 9 8 7 6 5 4 3 2 1

ISBN: 978-1-63159-272-0

Library of Congress Cataloging-in-Publication Data available

Translator: Namiji Hatsuse
Technical Editor: Jason Ku
English Editor: Lindsay Fair
Design: Arati Devasher, www.aratidevasher.com

Printed in China

BYE-BYE!